Brian Patten

Juggling
with Gerbils

Illustrated by Chris Riddell

PUFFIN BOOKS

PUFFIN BOOKS

Published by the Penguin Group
Penguin Books Ltd, 80 Strand, London WC2R 0RL, England
Penguin Putnam Inc., 375 Hudson Street, New York, New York 10014, USA
Penguin Books Australia Ltd, 250 Camberwell Road, Camberwell, Victoria 3124, Australia
Penguin Books Canada Ltd, 10 Alcorn Avenue, Toronto, Ontario, Canada M4V 3B2
Penguin Books India (P) Ltd, 11 Community Centre, Panchsheel Park, New Delhi – 110 017, India
Penguin Books (NZ) Ltd, Cnr Rosedale and Airborne Roads, Albany, Auckland, New Zealand
Penguin Books (South Africa) (Pty) Ltd, 24 Sturdee Avenue, Rosebank 2196, South Africa

Penguin Books Ltd, Registered Offices: 80 Strand, London WC2R 0RL, England

www.penguin.com

First published 2000
11

Text copyright © Brian Patten, 2000
Illustrations copyright © Chris Riddell, 2000
All rights reserved

The moral right of the author and illustrator has been asserted

Made and printed in England by Clays Ltd, St Ives plc

British Library Cataloguing in Publication Data
A CIP catalogue record for this book is available from the British Library

ISBN 0-141-30478-2

PUFFIN BOOKS

Juggling with Gerbils

Br‌‌ten was born in Liverpool. His poetry for adults has
b‌‌slated into many languages, and his collections include
L‌ms, Storm Damage, Grinning Jack and *Armada*. His verse for
c‌ includes *Gargling with Jelly, Thawing Frozen Frogs* and *The
‌utters*. Other books include *Jimmy Tag-along, Impossible
‌. The Magic Bicycle* and the award-winning novel, *Mr Moon's
L‌‌se*. Brian Patten is a popular performer of his work, and
h‌ also written children's plays as well as editing *The Puffin
‌Twentieth-Century Children's Verse*.

Contents

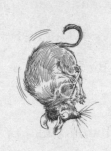

The Vampire Duck

There's a vampire duck waddling about,
You can hear its ghostly quack.
Keep away from the pond at midnight,
Or the feathery fiend will attack.

Odd Duck Out

It was really quite unnatural,
But a marvellous bit of luck
When on the banks of the River Thames
I saw a talking duck.

It stopped and said, 'Good morning,'
And asked me if I knew
Where it could find some chickens
To make some chicken stew.

'I thought you liked things cold,' I said,
'I thought you liked them raw.'
'I do, I do, I do,' it said,
And offered me its paw.

'I thought you had webbed feet,' I said,
'And hated chicken stew.'
'I do, I do, I do,' it said,
And then away it flew.

The Muscovy Duck

Early spring, and out on the misty river
The poor old Muscovite is lonely as ever.
Winter's buried its companion.
It swims behind the mallards
Or sits near them on the shore,
An old uncle with nowhere to go.

Tiger Shadows

I wish I was a tiger in the Indian jungle
The jungle would be my teacher

No school
And the night sky a blackboard smudged with stars
I wish I was a tiger in the Indian jungle

Kitten-curious
I'd pad about on paws big as frying pans

While the monkeys chatted in the trees above me
I'd sniff the damp jungly air
Out of exotic flowers I would make a crown of pollen

If I were a tiger in the Indian jungle
My eyes would glitter among the dark green leaves
My tail would twitch like a snake

I would discover abandoned cities
Where no human feet had trod for centuries

I would be lord of a lost civilization
And leap among the vine-covered ruins

I wish I was a tiger in the Indian jungle
As the evening fell
I'd hum quiet tiger-tunes to which the fireflies would dance

I'd watch the red, bubbling sun
Go fishing with its net of shadows

While the hunters looked for me miles and miles away
I'd lie stretched out in my secret den

I would doze in the strawberry-coloured light
Under the golden stripy shadows of the trees
I would dream a tiger's dream

The Day I Got My Finger Stuck up My Nose

When I got my finger stuck up my nose
I went to a doctor, who said,
'Nothing like this has happened before,
We will have to chop off your head.'

'It's only my finger stuck up my nose,
It's only my finger!' I said.
'I can see what it is,' the doctor replied,
'But we'll still have to chop off your head.'

He went to the cabinet. He took out an axe.
I watched with considerable dread.
'But it's only my finger stuck up my nose.
It's only a finger!' I said.

'Perhaps we can yank it out with a hook
Tied to some surgical thread.
Maybe we can try that,' he replied,
'Rather than chop off your head.'

'I'm never going to pick it again.
I've now learned my lesson,' I said.
'I won't stick my finger up my nose –
I'll stick it in my ear instead.'

A Boat in the Snow

On to the ocean's cold dark skin
Snowflakes are falling and are melting away.
How strange the snow seems out here!
How quickly the white blizzard is swallowed up by the waves.
Without the framework of land,
Each flake's transformed.
Like a trillion ocean-borne moths
They flick into existence, then go.
As the sky above and around me
Glitters with frosty flecks of stars,
So the deck of the boat glitters,
And I wonder, are whales sleeping
Out there in the world's depths, beyond
The boat's bow? And I wonder,
Do they really sleep? And how?
There is no one to ask.
Snuggled up in cabins
Passengers are dreaming,
And all round us still the snow is falling,
And the ship's deck has become
A moonlit field, a field adrift
On the dark skin of the world.
I would love to sail for ever between islands of snow.

Earwings

When I was little
My mother wore earwings.
Each night
She would creep to my bedroom window,
Open it,
And taking me gently in her arms
Glide off into the night.

Mr Dahl Supping Soup

He sat at the table supping his soup,
Like a big bear coaxed in from the wood,
He supped it without spilling a drop
Just as a grown-up should.

Nothing peculiar popped out of the soup,
No strange smells were hanging around.
He didn't pick his nose, pass wind or burp,
Or hover above the ground.

The waiter who served him wasn't a Twit,
Matilda was nowhere around,
And he sat looking normal supping soup
Without making the slightest sound.

The restaurant was unfazed by the famous
(Many a pop star supped soup there)
But there could have been a dozen pop stars,
The astonished kids didn't care,

For a man few grown-ups recognized
Sat big as a badly dressed bear,
Supping his soup without spilling a blob
Or getting it messed in his hair.

He looked surprisingly human
(With teeth that had seen better days)
And Mr Dahl sat supping his soup,
And the kids looked on in a daze.

My Neighbours' Rabbit

On the wall between my neighbours' garden and mine
a rabbit is sitting, shivering with cold.
They've been away some days now.
They've left out water and dry food
(though the rain's put paid to that).
What they haven't left behind is love.
They've asked no one to call in,
to stroke it, to make sure it's OK.
Having made it dependent upon them
they've abandoned it.
I take it from the wall,
feed it some apple, feel
how warm it grows, a furry volcano,
as warm as my absent neighbours are cold.
I marvel at how many sizes
the human heart comes in.
Some hearts have room inside them for a hutchful of rabbits,
some are so small
not even one rabbit would fit inside.
Perhaps my neighbours possess such hearts –
hearts that keep on shrinking,
that grow smaller and smaller until finally
nothing will fit inside, not even
the breath of a solitary rabbit.

Nature Adores a Good Vacuum

Saw Mother Nature
Zooming around
With a vacuum cleaner.
You should have seen her.
Her face was reflected
In every shiny surface.
Every pond and leaf
Glowed with light.
Everything was polished
As bright
As God's buttons.
Nature certainly
Adores a good vacuum.

Bringing up a Single Parent

It's tough bringing up a single parent.
They get really annoyed when they can't stay out late,
or when you complain about them acting soppy
over some nerdy new friend,
(even though you are doing it for their own good).
It's exhausting sometimes, the way you have to please them,
and do things you absolutely hate while pretending
it's exactly what you want.
Yep. Bringing up a single parent
is a real chore.
You don't get extra pocket money for them,
or special grants,
and you have to get up in the morning
and allow them to take you to school
so they can boast to their friends
about how clever you are.
And what's worse,
you have to allow them to fret over you,
otherwise they get terribly worried.
And if you're out doing something interesting after school
you have to keep popping home all the time
to check they're not getting up to any mischief
with a new friend, or smoking, or drinking too much.

You have to try and give single parents
that extra bit of attention.
But once you've got them trained,
with a bit of patience and fortitude
they're relatively easy to look after.
Still, it can be tough
bringing up a single parent.

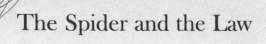

The Spider and the Law

'Spider, spider, you'll never catch
A hawk inside that web.'

'It's made for flies and not for hawks,'
Is what the spider said.

'Spider, spider, why is the law
So like a spider's web?'

'It catches flies, but not the hawks,'
Is what the spider said.

When you are called names, remember

If bullies mock and reject you
Repeat after the poet, please:
A cat's a wonderful creature
That does not converse with its fleas.

Never play cricket with rats because

Unfortunately unlike a ball
Rats do not seem to bounce at all.
One dull thud and they're a goner
(And you never score more than a one-er).

Freddy, the Vanishing Escapologist

Smooth-talking Freddy was ever so greasy,
You could never quite catch him however you tried.
He was sneaky and slippy and ever so nippy,
And pinning him down was terribly hard.
An expert at slipping away without warning
He was covered in butter and dripping and lard.
One day feeling ready to write about Freddy
I sat at my desk with paper and pen,
But the very moment I tried to begin
Fre

The Wet Goldfish

'I'm wet,' said the goldfish,
'Please bring me a towel,
Hurry, do as you're told!
I hate all this water
And think I have caught a
Bit of a chill or a cold.'
To the man who sold fish
I said that my goldfish
Was going mad in its bowl.
'It says it hates water
And thinks that I ought to
Go and fetch it a towel.'
'I suppose if you wish
To pamper goldfish
You ought to do as you're told.
But I honestly wish
I'd not sold you that fish,
For it seems quite a rare fish,
And I'd rather not sell fish
Worth double their weight in pure gold.'

Smart Alec

Smart Alec,
a crook
armed with a hook,
robbed riverbanks.
No matter how wide
they spread their nets
the police only
ever caught a
bit of water.

Geography Lesson

Our teacher told us one day he would leave
And sail across a warm blue sea
To places he had only known from maps,
And all his life had longed to be.

The house he lived in was narrow and grey
But in his mind's eye he could see
Sweet-scented jasmine clinging to the walls,
And green leaves burning on an orange tree.

He spoke of the lands he longed to visit,
Where it was never drab or cold.
I couldn't understand why he never left,
And shook off the school's stranglehold.

Then halfway through his final term
He took ill and never returned.
He never got to that place on the map
Where the green leaves of the orange trees burned.

The maps were redrawn on the classroom wall;
His name forgotten, he faded away.
But a lesson he never knew he taught
Is with me to this day.

I travel to where the green leaves burn,
To where the ocean's glass-clear and blue,
To places our teacher taught me to love –
And which he never knew.

Three Frazzles in a Frimple

1 snunk in a snuncle
2 gripes in a grimp,
3 frazzles in a frimple
4 blips in a blimp.
5 nips in a nimple
6 nerps in a neep,
7 gloops in a gloople
8 flurps in a fleap.
9 snozzles in a snoozle,
10 leaps in a bunny,
some sums are ridiculous
and some sums are funny.

The Mysterious Smirkle

Some say the Smirkle was a Smatterbug
And loved to smatterbug about,
But exactly what it was or did
We never did find out.

Was the Smirkle friendly?
Was it calm, meek and mild?
Or was it mean and nasty,
Belligerent and wild?

Did it live on cabbages,
Or did it live on Mars?
Was it made of chocolate drops,
Or formed by the light of stars?

It's one of Life's small mysteries
And gladly goes to show
There are still things left on the earth
That we will never know.

In the Jungle Restaurant

In among the green leaves,
Among the dangling vines,
All the hungry creatures
Were sitting down to dine.
'Lucy's juicy,'
said the tiger,
'Hughie's chewy,'
said the lion,
'Billy's chilly,'
said the panther,
'Won't you have a bit of mine?'
'Peter's pickled,'
said the rhino,
'Mary's hairy,'
said the shark,
'Andy's dandy,'
said the vulture,
'I found him in the park.'

'Freddie's ready,'
said the python,
'Daphne's dainty,'
said the fox,
'Rita's sweeter,'
said the cheetah,
'I stole her off the ox.'
'Chloe's doughy,'
said the raven,
'Sally's salty,'
said the bear.
'Sammy's tasteless,'
said the hippo,
'But I really don't care.'
'Ron's all gone,'
burped the wild pig,
'Except for the very ends.
But I'm still a little hungry –
Had he any friends?'

Uncle Joe and the Roman Centurions

My far-fetched Uncle Joe
Was a zillion years ahead of his time.
He sold Roman centurions
Anti-tank devices and sophisticated radar systems
It having slipped the centurions' minds
That tanks hadn't been invented,
And even ballistic missiles
Were still a long way off.

Scarce Rhymes

Sadly, in olden days
Poets couldn't rhyme
Caesar with freezer,
For though there were
Lots of Caesars
No one had
Electric freezers.
Likewise,
You couldn't rhyme
Wart or snort
With astronaut,
For back then
The human race
Didn't float about in space.

Lonely Rhymes

Without another sound to chime with,
rhymes are so lonely.
They trail behind poems
and seem at a loss,
orphans waiting in the margins,
hoping to be overheard
by another word.

How Do You Know I'm Me If You've Never Met Me?

I went into a room and asked a man I did not know,
'Are you sure you do not know me,
Are you sure it's me you do not know?'
'Yes, I've never seen you, you are someone I don't know,'
Said the man who'd never seen me and whom I did not know.
'If you've never seen me how on earth can you know
I am the same me as the me you do not know?'
That is what I asked the man who I did not know
But who knew I was the same me as the me he did not know.

The Soldier

Year in year out
through sun and snow
the statue watched
the school kids grow,
and wished it too
were flesh and bone
instead of dull
North Yorkshire stone.
Year in year out
it used to think
if only they
could see me blink,
if only they
could see me twitch,
trying my best
to scratch an itch.
If only I
for once could be
as lively as
a wind-blown tree.
Yet all I know
is that for me
stretches a stone
eternity.

With gun in hand
and old gas mask,
with cape and tack
and water flask,
here I stand guard
yet do not know
who is the friend
and who the foe.
The peace, the wars,
the heat, the snow,
the kids, the years,
they come and go.

The Delighted Fly

A fly landing on a statue's nose
Said, 'This human in repose
Is cold and still. It's quite a thrill
To walk on breathless lips
And unblinking eyes,
To cross fingers that do not itch
Or wish to crush;
To rest on an Adam's apple or
Circumnavigate without fear
The cool rim of an ear.
If all humans were like this I
Would be a happier fly.'

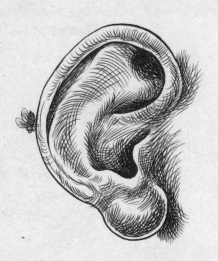

Bugs

The glow-worm and the dragon-fly,
The may-fly and lady-bird
Think that living near humankind
Is disgusting and absurd.

The centipede and millipede,
The spider, slug and snail
Think humankind's a murderous thing
And should be locked in jail.

But the bed bug, flea and cockroach,
The nit and tick and louse
Say humankind is quite OK
And like to share his house.

Billy Motor-mouth

Billy loved talking and didn't care who
The garbage he uttered was addressed to.
He'd jabber and gabber, whisper and wheeze
And say he was merely shooting the breeze.

Because silences gave Billy a fright
His tongue was active, morning and night.
He'd prattle and gossip, blather and shout,
But sadly his tongue never wore out.

Although Billy never meant to be rude
He'd spray us with words and small bits of food.
'Be quiet', 'Keep mum', 'Please hush', and 'Don't speak'
Were phrases he heard each day of the week.

What was it that kept his mouth on the go?
Had Billy eaten a small radio?
Listening to him, we used to puzzle
Why nobody had given Billy a muzzle.

Some people thought that he ought to be hung
Up in a tree by the length of his tongue.
But the thing that got us really unnerved
Was Billy believing he was reserved.

The Inside of Things

Inside the dandelion seed is a clock,
Inside the egg is a chicken farm;
Inside a fist an army awaits,
Inside a kiss is an open palm.

Inside a snowflake an avalanche
Trembles and waits to get free;
Inside a raindrop a river plots
The best way to run to the sea.

Not Only

Not only the leaf shivering with delight
No,
Not only the morning grass shrugging off the weight of frost
No,
Not only the wings of the crane fly consumed by fire
No,
Not only the steam rising from the horse's back
No,
Not only the sound of the sunflower roaring
No,
Not only the golden spider spinning
No,
Not only the cathedral window deep inside the raindrop
No,
Not only the door opening at the back of the clouds
No,
Not only flakes of light settling like snow
No,
Not only the sky as blue and smooth as an egg
No,
Not only these things

Vigil Virgil

Young Virgil stood vigil on top of a hill.
Said Virgil, 'I think I will be here until
I'm struck by an arrow or catch a bad chill.'
Though Virgil looks idle because he stands still
To stand vigil like Virgil requires great skill.
Few people stand vigil as well as Virgil
Stands vertically vigil on top of a hill.

Itchy Cat

Itchy cat, itchy cat where have you been?
To Buckingham Palace to sniff the Queen.
Itchy cat, itchy cat why do that?
Because I was chasing a right royal rat.
But I was polite and I said please,
And I came home with superior fleas.

Trees in the Storm

The trees cling to the earth with tired fingers.
No matter how the sky tugs at them
they cling and cling.
They wrap their roots around the rabbit's warren,
the badger's holt, the mole's tunnel,
and cling and cling,
and won't let go no matter what.
They are afraid of being torn free and hurled,
root and branch, into the black soup of the sky.

Most things cling to the earth,
Most things that are not balloons
or birds or dandelion seeds,
or bits of paper or smoke,
or kites or clouds,
cling to the earth.
Even shadows cling to the earth.
Stones do it best,
they are the experts.

But among living things
it is the trees,
swaying and rattling their heads,
branches snapping like bones,
each dishevelled twig wearing its necklaces of rain,
it is the trees
that fight so fiercely against the wild storm,
that cling and cling,
as if to life, as if never to give up.

A Warm Simile

In winter
Sitting by the fire
If you need
A simple simile
To keep the conversation simmering,
You could try saying,
It's as warm as toast,
Or,
If you want to make
A vegetarian sicken,
Try saying,
It's as warm as a roast chicken.

One of the Difficulties of Writing a Poem

On to the world's shoulders
Snow falls like dandruff

Snow falls like dandruff
On to the world's shoulders

Like dandruff, snow
Falls on to the world's shoulders

Snow, like dandruff, falls
On to the world's shoulders

On to the world's shoulders
Like dandruff, snow falls

Dandruff like snow
Falls on to the world's shoulders

On to the world's shoulders
Dandruff falls like snow

The Boy Who Broke Things

The boy kept breaking things.
He broke the one window through which the world
 looked bright.
He broke bottles,
He broke promises,
He broke his mother's heart.
He broke the lock on the cupboard
In which she kept the sky,
And so she floated away for ever.
He broke the lock on the box
In which his father kept the ocean.
His father was swept away and drowned,
And the boy never saw him again.
Angry, he stomped on the earth and tried to break it,
But it was a tough nut, the earth –
Far tougher than him.
Still, he left the grass blue with bruises
And the moles and worms
Came up to complain.
The boy tore the curtain that separated life from death,
And so he could no longer tell
What was alive inside him and what was dead.
He smashed the clues we use to separate fact from fiction,
And they became one thing to him.

His anger was like a nasty giant.
He was angry, but he could not say why
(Although he knew why, he could not say)
And the answer stuck in his throat.
It was a secret he did not want to keep,
  but could not get rid of.
And the bottled-up pain inside him
Was like a mad genie.

Something That Might Be Useful If You Are Ever Stranded on an Ice Floe

I have a umiak
(which as everyone knows
is the kind of boat sailed by Eskimos).

Neigh Manners

I'm in Mum's bad books again today.
Into the kitchen I've trampled hay,
And into the dining room – beg your pardon –
The stuff they use to improve the garden.

Remembering the Horse

The last time I saw the horse
It was standing in a field
As the last rays of sunlight ignited buttercups,

And light receded from the hedgerows,
Like a tide carrying on its hunched back
The flotsam of birdsong.

October 26th 2028

The astronomer, with a glint in his eye,
Looked through his telescope and sighed,
'If the asteroid doesn't miss us completely
We will be well and truly fried.

'For like a sponge made out of rough stones,
Like a scrubbing brush made of fire,
It's heading in our direction,
And the consequences could be dire.

'Still, it could miss us completely.
I really do hope that's the case,
For though by then I'll be long gone,
You'll still be gawping into space.

'And who knows what wonders might happen
As we stare out night after night.
The asteroid might suddenly vanish,
And an angel come into sight.'

Numerous new asteroids have been discovered recently. Many people believe one,
Asteroid XF11, will crash into Earth in 2028.

The Panther's Heart

Although he still pads about behind
The bars of his solitary cage,
Although he still looks up nightly
At the moonstruck mountains
And the falling snow,
The panther's heart
Stopped long ago.

A Moth in November

Poor old moth,
we mistook you
for a flake of ash,
a solitary scrap
blown about
by the wind.
Today's
a dark
cold day
in November,
but what use to you
the heat of the bonfire?

Curtains for Gran

Whenever some old friend of Gran's was mentioned,
Gran would say,
'It'll be curtains for her soon.'
I often wondered why
It was always curtains
Gran's friends were about to get,
And how come so many of her old chums
Had done without them for so long?
It really bothered me!
I tossed and turned all night
Worrying about all those poor people.
They must have had bare windows,
And been stared at by strangers year in, year out.
Imagine the trouble they must have had
Doing things like going to the toilet,
Or simply taking baths!
Getting undressed at night must have been a problem.
Did they walk about in the dark smashing into things,
Or did they brazen it out,
Stare defiantly out of their curtainless windows
At nosy parkers and casual passers-by?
It must have been very embarrassing.
I asked Gran to explain
Why so many of her friends

Were only just getting around to curtains,
Specially when they'd had all their lives to get them.
Gran said, 'Don't you be daft, you!
I'll explain later.'
But by the time later came
It was curtains for Gran.

Contrary Me

When I was little I wanted to know
Why the years passed so very slow.
Now I'm an adult, as they flash past
I want to know why they don't last.

The Gloomy Tortoise

A tortoise called Dorcas thought life ludicrous.
Carrying his own sarcophagus
His life felt endlessly posthumous.

I Really Do Not Mind the Zoo

I really do not mind the zoo.
I hate bars of course, but still, it's true
We're all fed regularly at the zoo.
Sometimes the penguins would like to go
To visit friends out in the snow.
The polar bears say it would be nice
To catch a view of polar ice.
But I think they're wrong. So would you,
If you got fed regularly at the zoo.
The lions say they would prefer their meat
Half-cooked by the savanna's heat.
But do they really know? Would you,
If you only ever ate at the zoo?
The cobra and the crocodile,
The alligator and the viper too
Say there's far better food outside.
But how do they know that's really true,
When they've never eaten outside the zoo?

I really do not mind the zoo.
I have my lunch there every day.
Sausage. Peas. Chips. A cup of tea.
At night I lock up, then go away
And leave the animals to dream
Of banquets that might have been.
Still, I don't feel bad. Would you,
If you ate regularly at the zoo?

The Snail and the Bird

Why did Nature make the snail so slow?
If it had no enemies I'd understand
Its lazy progress through the grass.
And how come some shells are as frail as glass?
Just now above the traffic roar I heard
A shell being smashed against a stone
By a seemingly bad-tempered bird.
So maybe shells are tougher than I thought.
But still, they can't be tough enough
To make much, if any, difference.
As usual the bird gets its food,
And flies off to its hungry brood.
Snails have been around so long
You'd think Nature would have had the time
To speed them up, or make their shells
Beak-proof against the birds. But no,
Nature leaves things as they are.
No doubt it knows best by far.
The once-hungry bird agrees,
And, well fed, whistles from the trees.

How Not to Approach a Cockroach

Never never
However meekly
Approach a cockroach
Obliquely

Jack Frost Is Playing Cards at the Roadside

Jack Frost
Is playing cards with the leaves.
He has spread them out in front of him
And is turning them over one by one,
Telling the Earth's fortune.
Which creatures
Will not wake from hibernation.
Which bulbs
Will burst with cold.
Which plants
Will melt away.
Jack Frost
Sits beside the roadside,
Lonely as ever.
On a twig behind him
A sparrow is sitting mute with cold,
And everything is still and quiet,
Still and quiet.

Across the valley is a village
And the roofs of its little houses
Steam in the morning light,
Which is cold and brief.
And over its inhabitants
Soon clouds will come,
And a net of shadows descend,
And Jack Frost
Will put away his cards,
And the whiteness will pass
And vanish from the grass.

'I'm Cold,' Said the Snowman

'I'm cold,' said the snowman, 'please bring me a coat,
And do light a fire at my side.
And a hot cup of tea sounds heaven to me,
And my gloves would be nice, if dried.'

But before I could say even on a cold day
A fire would be quite unwise,
The sun had come out and he was nowhere about –
Except for the coals of his eyes.

For a snowman's a no-man when touched by the sun,
He's a bye-bye-you-must-go-man for whom heat is no fun;
He's a handful of snowflakes that melt and are gone
While the wind blows around him and winter goes on.

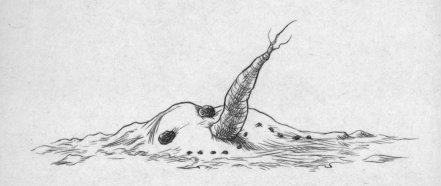

Batty Mrs Brown

Leathery-skinned Mrs Brown
Hung from the ceiling upside down.
Her next-door neighbour forced the door
And found bat droppings on the floor.
She said with glee, 'Just fancy that.
Old Mrs Brown's become a bat.'
Then Mrs Brown said with a scowl,
'Oh no, I'm not. I'm an owl.
And it would be extremely nice
If you went and fetched some mice.'

Milking a Bumblebee in the Rain

I tried to milk a bumblebee,
I was only after honey.
I'll try again another day
If it turns out sunny.

The Famous Five

Please speak to me, ears.
Give me the sound of water over stones.
And you too, eyes,
Don't hang around staring at the floor!
Show me again how in those far-off fields
The light falls like sheets of gold.
And nose, poor nose, subject of so many jokes,
Bring the scents of my childhood to haunt me:
The smell of privet hedges,
The tang
Of an estuary.
The scent of my mother's dress.
And you, touch,
Let me feel my friend's breath on my skin,
Falling there like a web of peace.
Tongue, remind me of what the earth tastes like.
And, while you're about it,
Tell me the words of the spell
That will stop the world from shrinking.
Ears, can you hear that spell?
Eyes, can you see if it's working?
Nose, please sniff out the truth.

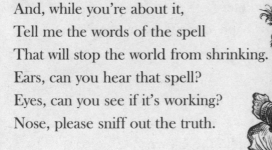

The Ghost of the Circus Clown

In the big top the ghost of a clown
Sits in a corner and sighs:
'I could have been a great acrobat –
Except for the tears in my eyes.

'I'd have been fantastic on the tightrope,
I'd have been great on the trapeze,
But the ringmaster withheld permission –
Because of the state of my knees.

'I'd have been wonderful with the horses,
Back-facing or riding free rein,
But whenever I tried to mount one
I felt a terrible pain.

'The lion's cage would have been no problem.
Old Leo would never attack.
But the circus doctor banned me from trying
Because of the pain in my back.'

It's not the wind whistling in the tent flaps,
It's not the bored animals' sighs,
It's only the ghost of Fibbo the Clown
Still telling his usual lies.

Usefully Useless

I asked him why he was building a fence
He asked me why
I thought he was building a fence

I said it's obviously a fence, just look
at all those planks

But it's not a fence he said
Look again
So I looked again
It is still a fence I said, it's those planks
give it away

See these gaps he said
Yes I said
The ones between the planks I said

Well he said I am using this wood
to build gaps for the wind
To blow through

I see I said

He said then why don't you
go and do
something useful too

OK I said, I'll build a box I said
What for he said

To put Nothing in I said

The Suspicious Detective

'I'm suspicious,' said the detective.
'I'm determined to solve this case.'
I insisted nothing had happened
Until I was blue in the face.

He insisted the crime was perfect.
He said it was driving him mad.
'The clues are as rare as the truth,' he said,
'And the alibis are iron-clad.

'The villain is obviously cunning
I won't let him escape from me.
The only reason for no witnesses
Is that none exist, you see.'

He said no other crime was as perfect.
For clueless, where could he begin
To find either a motive or suspect,
Or even the hint of a sin?

He said the evidence was baffling.
I said there was none to be had.
'That's exactly what I mean,' he said.
'That proves the crime is *really* bad.'

I was convinced nothing had happened,
And he was convinced that it had.
I was convinced the world was good,
And he was convinced it was bad.

The Awfullest of Friends

Alan shouts at Alice,
Alice snaps at Sue,
Sue scowls at William
(It's like living in a zoo).

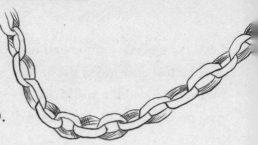

Andrew curses Sarah,
Sarah moans at John,
John despises Matthew
And wishes he was gone.

Jerry curses Tony,
Tony snarls at Tess,
Tess says Tina's boring
And that she looks a mess.

Sam finds Pete repulsive,
Pete thinks Josh is vile,
Josh says Gita's childish
And Patrick's infantile.

Edward jeers at Sadie,
Sadie laughs at Paul,
Paul says Zoe's stupid
And he hates them all.

I want to leave this party,
I'm not happy any more.
I used to like these people,
But now I'm not so sure.

Where Am I?

Am I in a place called Trouble,
Or is it called Disgrace?
Am I somewhere else entirely –
Perhaps in cyberspace?

Dad says I'm in Trouble,
Mum says I'm in Disgrace
(Secretly I'm in my room,
And refuse to show my face).

But no matter where they think I am
There's one thing I admit –
I've just broken Dad's computer,
And now I'm in for it.

A Valentine

A bushbaby's unhappy without its bush,
A grape without its vine,
A hulla's unhappy without a baloo
And a 'me' without a 'you're mine'.

A Poet I Know

I know a poet whose poems
Were told to shut up and wait.
They were impatient poems.

I know a poet whose poems
Hated everything.
They were lonely poems.

I know a poet whose poems
Were fed on blood.
They were angry poems.

I know a poet whose poems
Lived on thin air.
They were empty poems.

I know a poet whose poems
Were fed to him on a spoon.
They were lazy poems.

I know a poet whose poems
Told the best jokes in the world.
They were popular poems.

I know a poet whose poems
Lived on laughter and sunshine.
They were glorious poems.

I know a poet whose poems
Were the richest poems in the world.
They kept falling through the holes in his pockets.

The Mud Mother

With eyes of mud and a snail's tongue
She dines
On the corpses of otters, water rats and voles.
Her babies
Suckle mud from the riverbanks.
At night
She orders her brood to crawl up into boats,
And,
From the sleeping crew,
Steal a life or two.
If a river is tinged with red
You can bet
The Mud Mother lives there.
Her hair
Gets mistaken for the long green weeds,
Her voice
For the gurgling of water over stones.

Cerberus, the Dog

Cerberus is not a pet I would get.
Nor is it one I would let
Anywhere near me.
It's scary and hairy:
A three-headed hound,
Each head
The size of a football.
Each mouth
Reeking of decay.
Its six eyes
Red as burst tomatoes.
Its three tails
Coiling and hissing behind it.
If it broke free
One head would swallow the moon,
One head would swallow the sun,
One head would swallow the stars.
No, Cerberus is not
The kind of pet
I would get.

*In mythology, Cerberus is the monstrous watch-dog that guards the entrance
to the Underworld.*

The Yeti and the Monk

The monk said,
'In a mountain monastery when I was a child,
at the time of year when Everest
casts its shadow on the clouds
and plants push their way up through the powdery snow,
I knelt in the monastery garden among
the bright new blades of grass,
and a Yeti came and knelt beside me.
Swaying from side to side,
it pointed to the distant mountain as if to say,
"That is my home."
Then the creature rose,
and brushing my head with its gigantic paw,
wandered away sorrowfully across the snow.
Nothing else happened. It was a long time ago.'

The Misfit

The colour is draining from the grass,
The sky is heavy and it's getting dark,
And I'm still waiting outside the Ark.

'Noah,' I said, 'is there something I lack?'
'You are not a creature made by the Lord,
And without a mate you cannot come aboard.'

Stones stopped speaking and leaves held their breath,
In the old snake's eye was hardly a spark
As the gangplank was pulled into the Ark.

Far off across the desert I sniffed a dog bark.
I saw the colour of a song from the lark,
And I turned my two backs on that fool in the Ark.

'Nor has God a mate,' was my one retort
As Noah sailed off with the Devil aboard
In a different direction to his Lord.

The Secret Rhyme for Orange

Where's the secret rhyme for orange?
Is it lurking somewhere near?
Go and look under the sofa.
No? There's only grey fluff there?

Then where is that stupid rhyme?
I've been looking now for days!
Searching through the dictionary
Is like searching through a maze.

How can a word have no rhyme?
It really is not funny,
Orange is not a lonely word –
It's always seemed quite chummy.

You'd think if a word had no rhyme
It would be one like grim or bad,
Not a juicy word like orange –
It really makes me mad.

Look amongst the leaves of the orange tree.
See if the rhyme's sleeping there
Curled up in the branches
Without a worldly care.

Look in the caverns of the Sun,
Look on Jupiter and Mars.
If they've got a rhyme for orange
Bring it back. It's ours.

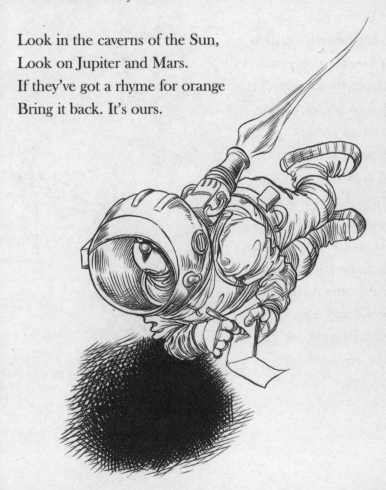

Fingers and Thumbs

When he dropped all the sweets
Harry said to his chums,
'Sorry about that,
I'm all fingers and thumbs.
If I drive a bargain
I immediately crash it,
If I hold a conversation
I immediately smash it.
A secret is something
I always let slip.
I can't take a journey
Without taking a trip.
If you lend me a hand
I immediately bruise it,
If you give me a minute
In an hour I'll lose it.
But I can take a hint,
So I'll stay away.
And I'll sit on my hands
The rest of the day.'

A Bun Dance

Have you ever seen a bun dance,
a bun dance,
a bun dance?
Yes, I've seen a bun dance,
a bun dance,
a bun dance.
Have you seen them dance in abandon,
abandon,
abandon?
No, only in abundance,
abundance,
abundance.

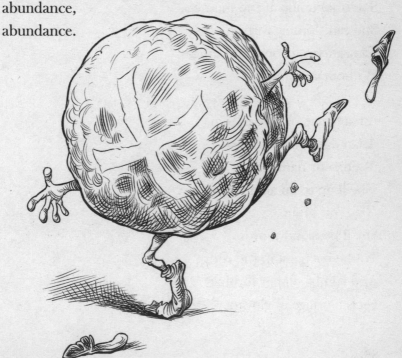

My Dancing Gran

People are talking rubbish
Especially if they say
At a hundred and one my old Gran
Can't dance the night away.

You want to see her Charleston,
You want to see her romp,
She'll leap around the furniture,
Or simply stand and stomp.

She's no jumbo at the mambo,
She can shimmy with the best,
She can samba on till midnight
Without a moment's rest.

A tea dance or a hoedown,
A fan dance or the twist,
A tango or flamenco –
(She'll do them all if asked).

She'll bossa nova over
To the youngest in the room
And rumba till her lumbar
Feels a twinge of gloom,

Then Gran'll do the cancan
And if the guests are still awake
She'll lead them in a conga line
And break-dance on a cake.

After a tot of sherry,
After wine with Sunday lunch,
After a nip of brandy
She's the wildest of the bunch.

Devil of a Dancer

This is the way the Devil dances:
He bangs on the drum of jealousy
The song he sings goes
me me me
His favourite sound is the raven's caw
me me me
more more more
He dances without passion
He dances without love
He tramples into pulp
The body of the dove
He dances like a rock
He dances like a stone
He dances in the darkness
He dances all alone
He plays his pipes with a snapped-off horn
He dances till the earth is torn
If you join his dance
You'll become oblivious
He can make you weep
Or feel quite hilarious.
He's envious and venomous
Viperous and poisonous
Yet when he plays his pipes

The tune sounds glorious
He's full of tricks and hocus-pocus
But can seem as fragile as a newborn crocus
He's the devil of a dancer and what's more –
He's dancing up to your back door.

The Word Spoken in Haste

You can catch the word hunt
You can dry the word wet
You can thaw the word frost
You can find the word lost
You can calm the word fright
You can light the word night
You can hush the word loud
You can plant the word seed
You can staunch the word bleed

Yet no matter what energy you waste
Nothing can catch the word spoken in haste

The Pecking Order

Charlie Chicken knew the pecking order,
He was as good as a good egg could be.
His father was tough and ruled the roost,
And it was plain for us all to see
Though they would never turn into swans
You couldn't fault them as poultry.

Geraniums in the Snow

Like children snuggling down under a white duvet
Slowly the red geraniums
Vanish under the snow.

What the Mountain Knows

It is the hare's breath melting the snow
causes the avalanche.

Thingamajigs

There's nothing dafter
Or causes more laughter
Than pigs in wigs
On thingamajigs.

Unfair

A giraffe's a giraffe
An ape is an ape,
But a pig is a sausage
In a different shape.

Bad Manners

It's extraordinary bad manners
And hard to justify
Picnicking near a pigpen
On spare ribs or pork pie.
You might be eating someone's granny,
Their father or their mum,
Those pork pies you're guzzling
Might be someone's chum.

In Tintagel Graveyard

In an ancient cemetery overlooking the sea, I saw fresh flowers that had been placed on the grave of a boy who had drowned more than a century ago.

Who brought flowers to this grave?
'I,' said the wren.
'I brought them as seeds and then
Watched them grow.'

'No,' said the wind. 'That's not true.
I blew them across the moor and sea,
I blew them up to the grave's door.
They were a gift from me.'

'They came of their own accord,'
Said the celandine.
'I know best. They're brothers of mine.'

'I am Death's friend,'
Said the crow. 'I ought to know.
I dropped them into the shadow of the leaning stone.
I brought the flowers.'

'No,' said Love,
'It was I who brought them,

'With the help of the wren's wing,
With the help of the wind's breath,
With the help of the celandine and the crow.

'It was I who brought them
For the living and the dead to share,
I was the force that put those flowers there.'

The Bird's Advice to the Astrologer

The astrologer will always fret and wonder
Just why his forecast was a blunder.

No matter what prophesies he made
Kingdoms blossomed and then decayed.

His instruments could not forecast
Who'd be the first to go; who last.

Then late one starry night he heard
This message from a singing bird,

'Not even a god forecasts the woe
Of all that comes to pass below.'

A Scarecrow in the Waves

Dressed in a sea captain's raggy jacket
Old straw-brains sways
In an ocean of frosty soil.

The seagulls ignore him.
The crows bob about
On the furrowed waves.

The distant trees are his masts,
The clouds his sails.

On the windblown horizon
The humpbacked hills
Sing like whales.

Feeding Time

Saw the baby
pouring porridge
over the clock.
It was feeding time.

The Forgetful Mother

My mother told me no nursery rhymes,
Not a single one.
By the time she remembered where she'd left me
My childhood had long gone.

Reading the Classics

The Secret Garden will never age;
The tangled undergrowth remains as fresh
As when the author put down her pen.
Its mysteries are as poignant now as then.

Though Time's a thief it cannot thieve
One page from the world of make-believe.

On the track the Railway Children wait;
Alice still goes back and forth through the glass;
In Tom's Midnight Garden Time unfurls,
And children still discover secret worlds.

At the Gates of Dawn Pan plays his pipes;
Mole and Ratty still float in awe downstream.
The weasels watch, hidden in the grass.
None cares how quickly human years pass.

Though Time's a thief it cannot thieve
One page from the world of make-believe.

The Neighbour Without a Shadow

We never saw our neighbour in the daylight.
No one did. Some kids even doubted his existence.
No one lives in that house, they'd whisper,
staring at number forty with its unpainted door
endlessly closed and its grubby windows,
and velvet curtains thick with dust.
And you might have believed them
but for the sound of footsteps in the parlour,
and the nightly scraping of something
terrible being pulled across the floor.
He was there all right, despite the fact
that even on the frostiest nights
no smoke rose from his chimney,
despite the fact that no one ever called –
no postman, no milkman, no friends.
No one delivered even the barest necessities to his house,
But he was there, planning his plans,
biding his time. Shadowless,
sitting upright in the darkness,
smiling his skeletal smile
as the months and the years passed,
and people came and went,
whispering and doubting his existence,
just as he intended.

Our Sister, the Mad Scientist

A doctor? A surgeon? A world-famous vet?
What would Chloe be? We didn't know yet.
But up in the attic she couldn't resist
Playing at being a mad scientist.

Up in that room germs hadn't a hope
As she scrubbed away with carbolic soap.
With plastic knives, scissors, and bits of old string
She was about to dissect The Terrible Thing.

With legs like a frog and a head like an owl,
With bulging eyes and a childish scowl,
With a tongue like a slug and a smell like a bin
The Thing looked like her brother, James Albert Finn.

Looked like her brother? No – it really *was* him,
Tied up on the table creating a din.
We rushed up to the attic just in time.
To stop Chloe committing a terrible crime.

'I just wanted to look inside his daft head
To see what kind of rubbish existed,' she said.
'We could have saved you the trouble,' we sighed,
'For James's head has nothing inside.'

To a Boy Who Shot at a Bird

If you separate a robin from its wing
Or a bumblebee from its sting
Then these things cease to be,
And nature fills with misery,
And no doubt you will find
One day the wing will sting your mind.

The Bird Table

Grandad's old bird table
Dragged more birds down out the sky
Than a cat ever dreamed of.
I try to conjure up how it looked when new,
But fail, and see only an upright pole, the broken table
Dangling ghost-pale in a corner.
Abandoned now beneath the green dust of a birch tree
It seems so old and useless.
Yet once it reached up, exulting in a feast of crumbs,
Its wooden palm open to heaven.
If birds had a sense of history,
What would they make of it?
A sacrificial altar elbowed aside by time?
A monolith supporting the legend of how once
There was a world of plenty?
A time when Bird and Man
Spoke one tongue, exchanged gifts.
Song for bread. Bread for song.

Mr Ifonly

Mr Ifonly
Sat down and he sighed,
'I could have done more,
If only I'd tried.

'If only I'd followed
My true intent,
If only I'd said
the things that I meant.

'If only I'd gone
And not stayed at home,
If only I'd taken
The chance to roam.

'If only I'd done
As much as I could,
And not simply done
The things that I should.

'If only a day
Had lasted a year,
If only I'd lived
Without constant fear.

'Now life's passed me by
And it's such a crime,'
Said Mr Ifonly,
Who'd run out of time.

Juggling with Gerbils

Don't juggle with a gerbil
No matter what the thrill
For gerbils when they're juggled
Can end up feeling ill.
It makes them all bad tempered
And then they'd like to kill
Those gerbil-juggling jugglers
Juggling gerbils till they're ill.

(Do not try this at home.)

Index of First Lines